Fun with Abby & Alyssa ™

An Introduction to Sign Language

A day at School

Written by Grandpa Don ™
Illustrated by Liam Gooley

Written by Grandpa Don
Illustrated by Liam Gooley

Fun With Abby and Alyssa
A day at School
Copyright @ 2011 by Donald McNamara

Illustrations Copyright @ 2011 by Donald McNamara

ISBN#: 978-0-9833163-4-3

Dedication

Abby and Alyssa are real people. They both have significant medical challenges and use sign language to talk. As growing sisters, their energy and charisma can be inspirational to anyone that wishes to learn.

This series of books is dedicated to Abby and Alyssa who inspire me, and to Grandma Gina who lives on within our hearts.

Grandpa Don ™

Hi! My name is Abby and this is my sister Alyssa.

Alyssa uses signs instead of words to talk. She makes these signs with her hands.

You already know some signs like waving your hand to say hi.

Come with us to school and we'll learn more signs!

Hi: **Open hand waved side to side.**

There are signs for many things, like "school".

Let's see what we find at school and sign them together!

School: Tap the fingers of the right open hand, palm down, on the upturned palm of the left open hand twice.

What do we ride to school?

Let's all make the sign for bus!

Bus: Place the little finger of the right "B" hand on the index finger of the left "B" hand, palms facing opposite directions, move right hand back towards right shoulder.

This is Ms. Jones. Can you guess who she is?

The Sign: Move both flattened "O" hands away from forehead twice. Then move both open hands, palms facing, down along each side of the body.

Let's all make the sign for teacher!

What does our teacher use to read stories to us?

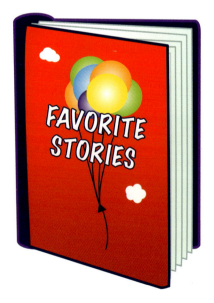

The Sign: Palms together in front of body with fingers pointed forward, bring hands apart at the top while keeping little fingers together.

That's right, our teacher reads stories from a book!

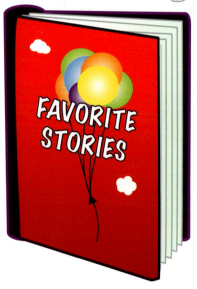

Let's all make the sign for book!

Book: Palms together in front of body with fingers pointed forward, bring hands apart at the top while keeping little fingers together.

What do we use to color?

Let's all make the sign for crayons!

Crayons: Rub the extended right little finger, palm facing down, back and forth on the left open palm twice.

What do we draw on with our crayons?

The Sign: Brush the heel of the right open hand, palm down, on the heel of the left open hand, palm up, twice.

Let's all make the sign for paper!

Paper: Brush the heel of the right open hand, palm down, on the heel of the left open hand, palm up, twice.

What do we eat at school?

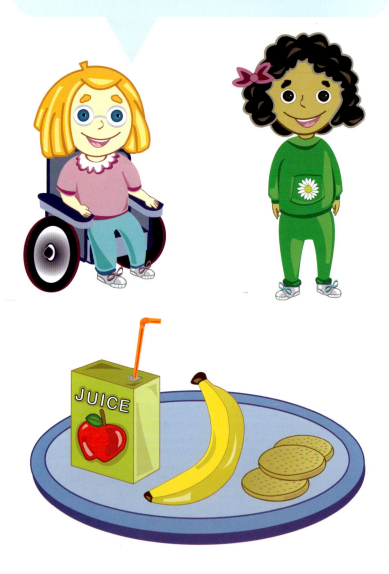

The Sign: Move the fingertips of the right "F" hand from touching the left open palm in front of chest, palms facing, upward to the mouth twice.

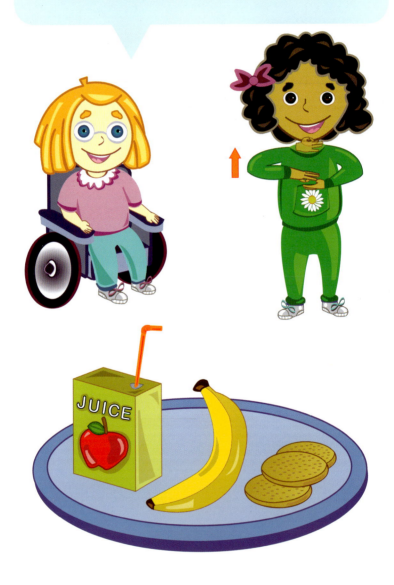

Let's all make the sign for snack!

Snack: Move the fingertips of the right "F" hand from touching the left open palm in front of chest, palms facing, upward to the mouth twice.

We've learned
a lot of signs about
school today.

It's time for
Alyssa and me
to go home...

Let's all make the sign for good-bye!

Good-Bye: Wave open hand up and down.

For more fun with sign language, you can practice your A,B,C's and numbers!

alphabet

A

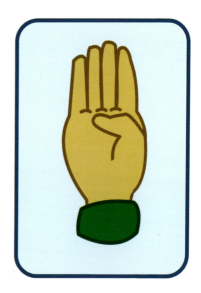

B

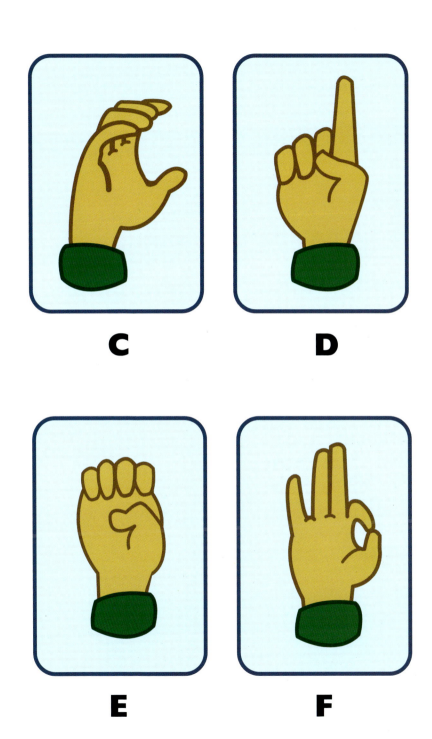

C

D

E

F

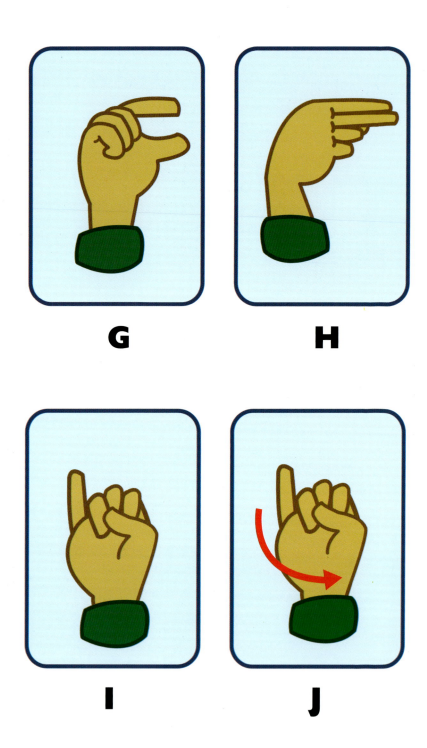

G

H

I

J

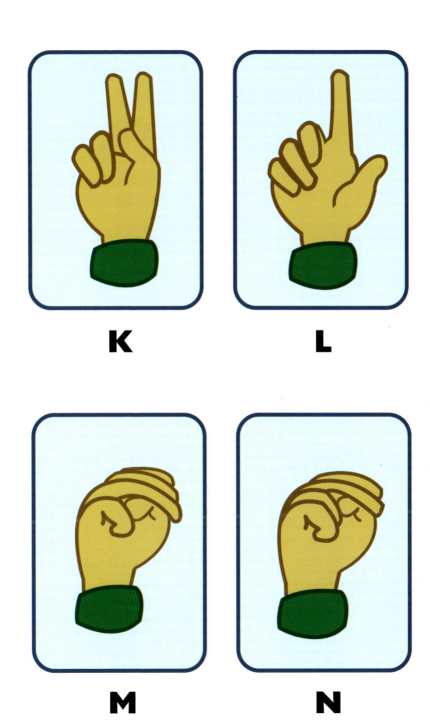

K

L

M

N

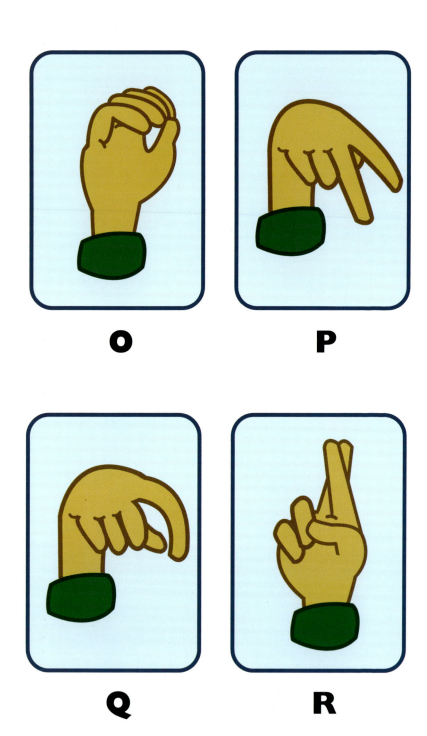

O

P

Q

R

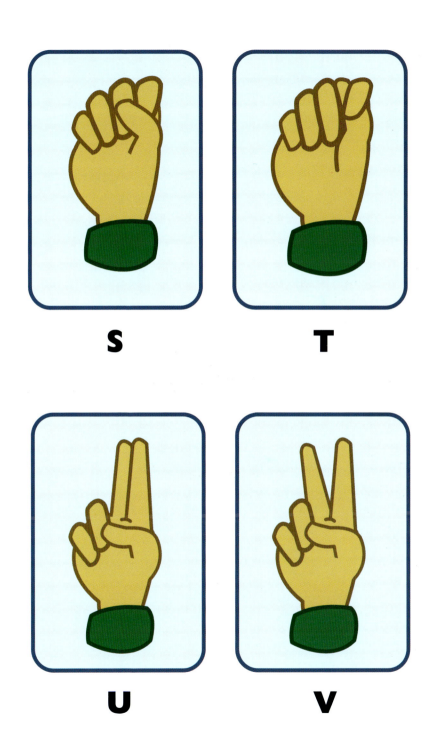

S

T

U

V

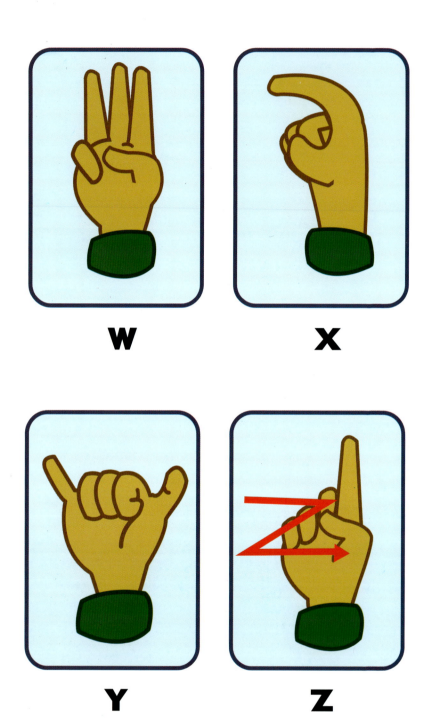

W   X

Y   Z

numbers 1 - 10

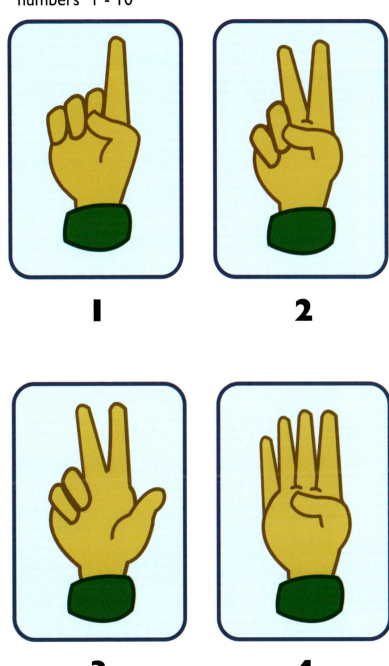

1

2

3

4

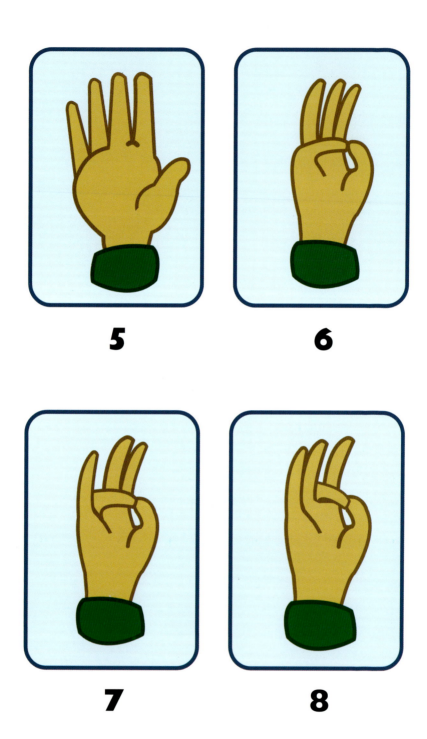

5

6

7

8

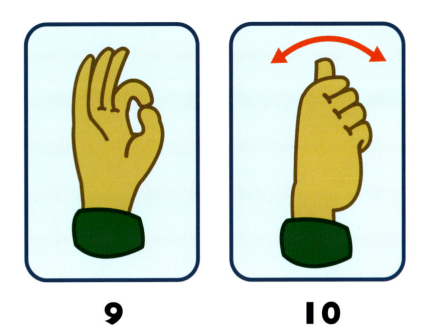

9   10

Acknowledgements

Some words in sign language have multiple acceptable signs. In those instances where multiple signs were available, Grandpa Don ™ chose the sign most appropriate for Abby and Alyssa.

Grandpa Don ™ encourages readers who want to learn more about sign language to read:

• "The Art of Sign Language" by
  Christopher Brown; Random House.

• "Webster's Unabridged American
  Sign Language Dictionary" by Elaine Costello, PHD.

And to also visit these websites:

• www.signingsavvy.com

• www.lessontutor.com